# NEW ZEALAND IN COLOUR

# NEW ZEALAND
## IN COLOUR

PHOTOGRAPHS BY
KENNETH AND JEAN BIGWOOD

TEXT BY JAMES K. BAXTER

## A. H. & A. W. REED
WELLINGTON   AUCKLAND   SYDNEY

First published 1962
Reissued 1962, 1963, 1965, and 1966
**Reissued edition 1967**


A. H. & A. W. REED
182 Wakefield Street, Wellington
**29 Dacre Street, Auckland**
51 Whiting Street, Artarmon, New South Wales




© A. H. & A. W. REED

**KYODO PRINTING COMPANY LTD. TOKYO JAPAN**

# INTRODUCTION

THIS BOOK invites you to make a journey. You may of course treat it, if you wish, as a random collection of photographs, to thumb through on a wet Saturday afternoon. But those who obtained the pictures, selected them, and added a written comment, had something more in mind. A pattern emerges from the series—not imposed by photographer or writer, but there from the beginning—the face of the country itself, at times domesticated and respectable, at times the face of a primeval goddess, pitted by the sun, by earthquake and the waves of the sea. This book invites you to explore this pattern and come one step nearer to seeing New Zealand as she actually is.

Writing about the island of Rhodes, Lawrence Durrell mentions the mysterious disease of "islomania"—those who suffer from it are pulled towards islands as if by a magnet. The mere fact of being on a small piece of land surrounded by water fills them with a lasting exhilaration. Any New Zealander, whether one by birth or by adoption, who cuts the navel-cord that binds him to England or Europe, and lives his life through on the terms that these islands dictate to him, is probably in Durrell's sense an "islomane". In his poem, "Dominion", A.R.D. Fairburn has recorded the sea-change endured by the first European immigrants....

> In the first days, in the forgotten calendars,
> came the seeds of the race, the forerunners:
> offshoots, outcasts, entrepreneurs,
> architects of Empire, romantic adventurers;
> and the famished, the multitude of the poor;
> crossed parallels of boredom, tropics
> of hope and fear, losing the pole-star, suffering
> world of water, chaos of wind and sunlight,
> and the formless image in the mind;
> sailed under Capricorn to see for ever
> the arc of the sun to northward...

Those first architects and adventurers carried in their minds an image of the society which they desired to create. A Utopia, a Happy Island, a Just City, in which the best of the Old World would survive, taking new antipodean forms. And though all Utopias are countries of the mind, their actual achievement was not negligible. Our difficult balance of power between labour and management, our early universal franchise, our legal equality of Polynesian and European, our state welfare for the young and the sick and the aged, have developed by degrees from their original foundation.

You can get a clear enough idea of the human acts of the past hundred years from any New Zealand history book. A City of a kind has been made. The hydro-electric dams at Roxburgh or Mangakino, the productive farms in place of endless tussock or bush, the tidy townships, the suburbs that climb hill-slopes towards the sun, and the honeycomb of factory and office buildings where each man has his appointed job under the eye of the clock—these are the works of the City, finite, exact and reasonable, designed for the fulfilment of limited aims. But alongside the human City, indifferent or even hostile, remains the Wilderness, whose time is still that of the sixth day of creation and whose works belong to the Power that created her.

It would have been possible for this book to have been a record of industrial, agricultural and technological achievement in New Zealand; and perhaps it would have pleased those readers who hold that the Wilderness exists only to be subjugated and contained within the pattern of the City. Instead of cities, towns and settlements, we have chosen to reveal mainly the natural features of the country, sometimes where they meet the City, but more often where they compose the Wilderness of lonely coast or mountains; and our comment includes references to Maori legend and quotations from contemporary New Zealand poets. On its own the City does not readily engender works of art. At the fringes of the human domain, where the City encounters the Wilderness, artists are able to discover those forms which become the treasures of their race, and the real knowledge which liberates the intellect...

Consider this barbarian coast,
Traveller, you who have lost
Lover or friend. It has never made
Anything out of anything.
Drink at these bitter springs...

This gullied mounded earth, tonned
With silence, and the sun's gaze
On a choir of breakers, has outgrown
The pain of love. Drink,
Traveller, at these pure springs...

The City is never truly self-sufficient, for it possesses only the power to use and organise a world which it has not created. Perhaps the Maoris, to whom many references are made in these pages, attributing spiritual powers to the Wilderness, refusing to fell a tree until the deities of the bush had been propitiated, were wiser than their European successors. The springs of thought and feeling did not dry up in them, and they have remained to a large degree unruled by the stiff hands of a clock. A very few Pakehas also—fishermen, deer-cullers, back-country shepherds, gold prospectors—have established a true relation to the Wilderness and been able to inhabit the country they were born in. To such men this book would seem unnecessary; for they already know all it could show them.

To others it may bring a composite impression of a country not long settled by Europeans, whose predominant colour is the green of farm and bushland, a country without smog, whose people, industrious by habit, have a great potential freedom, since few of them have ever known hard poverty. The journey which you may follow, through the pages of this book, begins at a lonely cape on the tip of the North Island and ends in the extreme south. Its time pattern commences in the spring of one year and concludes in the early winter of the next. Let the photographs tell their own story.

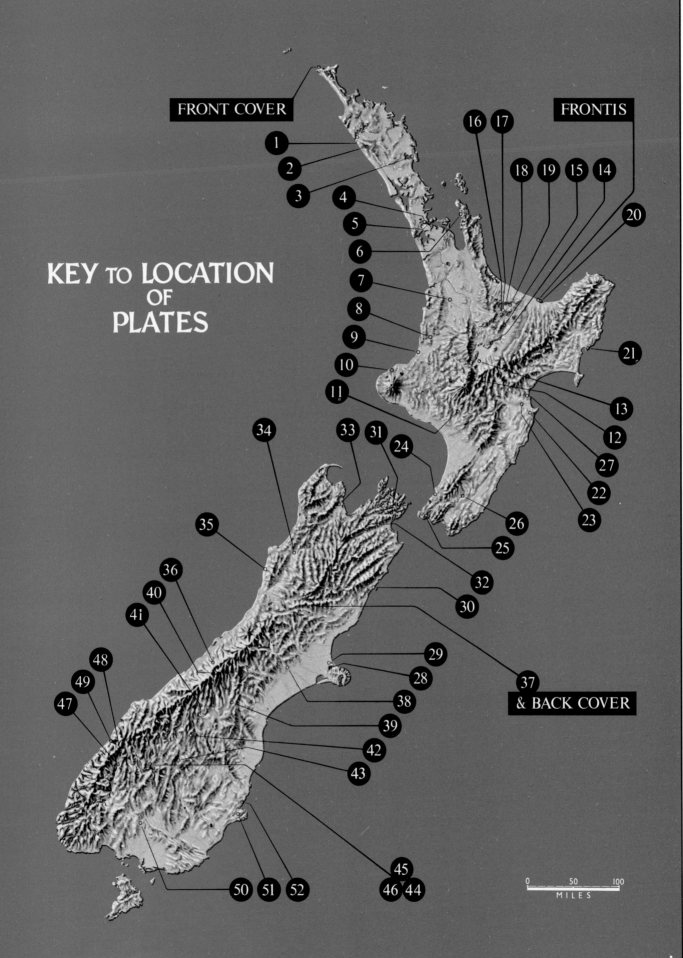

KEY TO LOCATION
OF
PLATES

FRONT COVER

FRONTIS

& BACK COVER

0    50    100
MILES

FROM a steep cliff at Cape Reinga, according to Maori belief, the spirits of the dead set out on their journey across the landless waters to Hawaiki. Now there is a lighthouse to guide the living sailors. You will find a picture of the cape, half-screened by slender *toetoe* plumes, on the dust-jacket of this book. The spirits, as they passed north, knotted the sandhill grasses to leave a memento behind them.

Facing this page you can see Omapere Bay, in Hokianga Harbour, with many-headed New Zealand cabbage-trees in the foreground. The tender shoots of the cabbage-tree can be cooked and eaten, and they taste like acrid leeks. On the shoreline grow mangroves, ankle-deep in the tide. It is a rough bush-clad country, where the land is still farmed by Maoris . . .

In houses thatched with nikau palm,
    Fearing the dead, riding bareback
On hill stallions, those who learned before us
    The secret of survival, to be patient
Suffer, and shut no doors,
    Change all things to their habit, bridge
The bogs with branch laid to branch . . .

PLATE 1
Looking inland from above Omapere Bay,
Hokianga Harbour, Northland.

THIS is the motor road through the Waipoua Kauri Forest, Northland, with the Waikohatu Stream in the foreground. The best-known of the larger trees is "Tane-Mahuta", reached by a short track from the roadside about forty miles north of Dargaville—a true giant with a girth of forty-three feet, not less than twelve hundred years old. The kauri logs make good ships' timber, and the timber trade began early in New Zealand, when Captain Dell, master on the *Fancy,* made contact with the Maoris in 1794 . . .

> . . . the Navy needed clean tall trees
>     And the forests where they throve
> Cook had seen in those savage lands,
>     So I risked a secret move
> And on a blue September morning
>     Made sail from Sydney Cove . . .

So Gloria Rawlinson writes in her ballad, "Captain Dell of the Fancy". Many kauris were chopped down, and others destroyed in the fires by which the first European settlers cleared the land. Gum-diggers came to probe the earth for the hardened blood of the kauris, the valuable resin. You can find in our museums spiders and other insects embalmed, perfect as in life, in the amber gum-stones. But Waipoua is now the last extensive tract of kauri forest left in New Zealand.

PLATE 2
Kauri trees by the road, Waipoua Forest, Northland.

PARUA BAY, an inlet on the northern shore of Whanga-rei Harbour, is a place for camping and bathing and fishing, and sport can be had with big game fish at Tutu-kaka on the Pacific coast beyond the Whangarei Heads, visible in the background of this picture. Over a century ago a sawmill was established in the bay, on the island of Motuki-ore ("Isle of the Rat"), and today one can still imagine a schooner riding at anchor in the estuary, while her holds and deck are loaded with kauri timber for the shipyards of Sydney. But the stands of kauri have long since gone, and sheep now graze on the level paddocks beside the harbour.

Above Whangarei Heads stands the curiously shaped peak of Manaia. Its name is the same as that of the human figure with bird-like features which appears on the carved barge-boards of Maori meeting-houses.

PLATE 3
View overlooking Parua Bay, towards
Whangarei Heads, Northland.

THE city of Auckland looks almost pastoral, seen from the slopes of Mount Eden, with the island of Rangitoto (another extinct volcanic cone—the city is pimpled with them) visible in the background. Yet Mount Eden was once the scene of many tribal battles.

The Aucklanders are by habit less inhibited than their southern neighbours. Perhaps it is the climate. In sunny weather Queen Street swarms with tanned legs and coloured dresses and headgear. Or perhaps it is the wind from the vineyards that surround the city, many of them owned by Dalmatian settlers. A.R.D. Fairburn, an Aucklander, caught something of the spirit of the town in his ballad, "Down on My Luck" . . .

Wandering above a sea of glass
in the soft April weather,
wandering through the yellow grass
where the sheep stand and blether;
roaming the cliffs in the morning light,
hearing the gulls that cry there,
not knowing where I'll sleep tonight,
not much caring either . . .

A city of extremes, where thunder-showers drop suddenly from what has been a clear sky; a place of alternate vigour and exhaustion, of sprawling streets and a thousand bays.

PLATE 4
Auckland City and Rangitoto Island
from Mt. Eden.

THE yachts move out, with spinnakers hard as drums, across the ruffled waters of Auckland Harbour. In the background is seen the arched bridge that joins the North Shore to Westhaven—another reminder of the likeness between Auckland and Sydney.

Some ferries still cross the harbour. It will be a pity when they all go out of fashion. Many people have had the experience of coming from a labyrinth of streets on to the wharves, on a day when the sun sits in a sky of brass, for the cool respite of a ferry trip to a friend's house at Devonport; or crossed with fear and exhilaration on a night when the ferry bucked like a horse, spray breaking over her bows.

But even if the ferries go, the yachts will remain. With centreboards or keels, brand-new sails or patched ones, they skim like mollymawks on a summer day over the sea that invades the town. It must be worth the pains of growing up to be young in Auckland.

PLATE 5
Yachting on Waitemata Harbour,
Auckland.

LITTLE islands flock along the Coromandel coast, due east and forty sea miles from Auckland. The peninsula, the mountain range, the eastern harbour and its township—all bear the exotic Indian name of Coromandel. Bush still covers much of the high hill-country, and the roads wind round unexpected bends and up impossible spurs. Holiday-makers swarm out from Auckland in summer to camp in the warm coastal bays.

Gold first brought the European settlers to Coromandel, but the claims were soon worked out. The shafts have long since fallen in, but the batteries that stamped the gold out of the ore still rust there, gripped by vines in the silent bush.

Rock oysters grow at Amodeo Bay, nine miles north by road from Coromandel, beached with gravel like many similar bays on this side of the peninsula, and sheltered by red-flowered pohutukawas. In the foreground appear the stately nikau palms, whose leaves have served to thatch many a Maori whare and settler's hut.

PLATE 6
Nikau palms near Amodeo Bay on the
Coromandel-Colville road.

THIS dairy herd is grazing in the paddocks of the Mangapiko district, under the slopes of Mount Pirongia. The New Zealand farmers, self-reliant men, claim often that they are the backbone of the country. Certainly they have changed its face and made the bush lands into fertile pastures. Barry Mitcalfe has celebrated the harsher side of farm life in his poem, "Sharemilkers" . . .

Bog-slow . . . as if the mud
Had never let them go, they are moved
Through Friday town and Sunday church . . . .

An old bull bugles at the boundary-gate
But the cows—secure in their season and
    stone-walled
Kingdom of grass—are not concerned;
Only the woman gazes dully out,

While her husband ploughs and sows
The slow hills with his seed.

But the farm in the picture is probably more prosperous than the one sketched in Mitcalfe's poem. The farmer may own a new Zephyr and his wife may attend adult education classes in the nearest town.

PLATE 7
Dairy herd and farmlands near Te Awamutu in the Waikato district.

THESE limestone outcrops, like the walls of a medieval castle, occur frequently in the country from northern Taranaki to the outlet of the Waikato River, south of Auckland city. In the limestone country, underground water makes caves and potholes, some of which may still be undiscovered, though the most famous caverns have been developed as a tourist attraction at Waitomo.

This photograph was taken at Mahoenui, on the Awakino Gorge road between Te Kuiti and New Plymouth, a road that follows the twists of the Awakino River to the sea. The name Mahoenui refers to the "large mahoe trees" of a densely forested region that has had to give ground to the grasslands of the farmers. Near this place a natural bridge of limestone spans the deep bed of the river. At either end of the arch stand ancient sites of Maori pas, reminders of the days when each Maori settlement was built on some high place hard for attackers to scale, and guarded by deep ditches and strong palisades.

PLATE 8
Limestone outcrops beside the Te Kuiti-New Plymouth highway near Mahoenui.

THE cliffs at Tongaporutu crumble slowly before the winds and waves that beat in from the stormy Tasman Sea. Their white limestone foreheads are turned to the west, contrasting with the black ironsand beach below them.

It was at the mouth of the Tongaporutu River that the *Tokomaru* canoe of the "Maori fleet" made its final landfall after the arduous journey from the homeland of Hawaiki, near Tahiti, more than six centuries ago. The name Tongaporutu may well refer to the hour of arrival, for it can be freely translated as "the head-on butting (of the canoe) into a southerly gale at night".

Each of the fleet canoes ended its journey at a different part of the New Zealand coast, and settlement spread inland and southwards. The Ngati-Tama tribe of these parts, descendants of the seafarers in the *Tokomaru,* were warlike in the extreme and eventually suffered defeat and expulsion at the hands of their enemies.

PLATE 9
Looking north from Tongaporutu in the
North Taranaki Bight.

HERE Mount Egmont is clearly visible from Churchill Heights, New Plymouth. An extinct volcano of almost perfect proportions, this mountain stands alone above the spreading slopes of Taranaki province, much as Fujiyama dominates its surrounding countryside in Japan. Captain Cook and his ship's company sighted the mountain in 1770, and he described it as "...a very high mountain and in appearance resembling the Peak of Teneriffe..." It is over 8,000 feet in height, bush-clad to the winter snowline and capped by snow and ice except in the warmth of summer, and it draws rain to many of the dairy farms that lie near its base. It has proved dangerous to mountaineers, who are misled by its deceptively easy slopes, where the snow can harden in an hour to ice. The Maoris regarded the mountain as a holy place.

New Plymouth, less than twenty miles north of the mountain, was settled first by whalers at Ngamotu Beach in 1828. At Pukekura Park there is a small lake set among trees and ferns, and a sportsground in a natural amphitheatre. New Plymouth is the seaport for the Taranaki dairylands.

PLATE 10
Mt. Egmont from Churchill Heights, Westown, New Plymouth.

H ERE the Raukawa Falls, on the Mangawhero River, are seen from the Parapara Road, until recently a route of fabled difficulty for the motorist, but now a high-speed link between National Park and Wanganui. The road follows part of the Mangawhero River, which rises as a trickling stream almost 8,000 feet up on the slopes of Mount Ruapehu, losing its identity when it joins the Whangaehu a short distance above Ngaturi.

Cataracts such as this may be found on many New Zealand rivers, where earthquakes have raised or lowered the level of the country. In this picture autumn leaves add their colour to the green of the bushland.

PLATE 11
Raukawa Falls on the Mangawhero River,
between Raetihi and Wanganui.

ABOVE the water-worn boulders of the Whakapapanui River and the wastelands of the central pumice plateau, stands the active volcano, Mount Ngauruhoe. Situated between Tongariro to the north and Ruapehu to the south, Ngauruhoe is one of the three major volcanic peaks of the Tongariro National Park. Here fire and ice lie close together, divided by barriers of rock. In winter, visitors come for skiing to the Chateau Tongariro. Passing by car on the swift road across the plateau, you may see Ngauruhoe, when she is active, simmering like a gigantic tea-kettle by day, or shooting up white-hot stones like tracer bullets at night. But there is no real danger involved, except perhaps for the seismologist who goes inside the lip of her crater.

The Maoris regarded these three mountains as guardian deities. There is a legend to the effect that Ruapehu, Tongariro, Ngauruhoe and Taranaki (the Maori name for Mount Egmont) were once grouped together, but that Taranaki departed to his present position because of a domestic quarrel.

PLATE 12
Mt. Ngauruhoe and the Whakapapanui River,
Tongariro National Park.

THIS view looks across Lake Taupo, New Zealand's largest sheet of fresh water, from Mission Bay, towards the National Park mountains. In ancient times Motutaiko Island in Lake Taupo was a Maori burial place, and some of the interment caves can still be seen there. Pohutukawa trees grow on the island but, according to the Maoris, do not grow naturally anywhere else around Lake Taupo. The Tongariro River flows into Taupo by a delta of five mouths. The waters of the lake occupy a depression caused by volcanic agency, and many streams enter it from all sides.

At the head of the Tapuaehururu Bay, where the Waikato River leaves the lake, stands the township of Taupo. It is a town built largely round the tourist trade, with hotels and motels, launches for hire, trout-fishing facilities, and intense thermal activity at Wairakei, where the sources of natural steam have been tapped to provide power. It is best perhaps in this area to travel by car and find one's own camping-ground in one of the secluded places.

Springtime at Taupo sees flowering kowhai massed along parts of the lake shore and the mountains of Tongariro National Park, Ruapehu especially, still carrying a thick coat of snow.

PLATE 13
Looking across Lake Taupo from Mission Bay to the Tongariro National Park mountains.

THE word *huka* itself means "foam". The Huka Falls, on the Waikato River, can be reached by side road from a turn-off three miles beyond Taupo. Here the river, hemmed in by a narrow rocky cleft, pours out from the giant's bath that is Lake Taupo, to drop more than thirty feet. This view is seen from the easily accessible look-out point provided for passing motorists. But if you have strong nerves, you can go over a narrow wooden foot-bridge just above the falls, and see them closely from many angles. The roar is continuous.

Downstream from Wairakei, the river plunges through the Aratiatia Rapids, where a dam is being built to harness it for hydro-electric power. Here too there are well-fenced look-outs high on the bluffs. The river discharges more than 800,000 cubic feet per minute. At various places hydro-electric stations have already been constructed, taming stretches of foaming rapids and replacing them with deep green lakes, where motor-boats troll for trout or haul water-skiers behind them in endless curves.

PLATE 14
The Huka Falls on the Waikato River
at Wairakei.

THE name Waiotapu means "sacred waters". At this thermal resort, eighteen miles from Rotorua, there are a geyser and several other spectacles, including Frying Pan Flat and Green Lake, which are visible in this picture. To the north-east of Waiotapu stands Rainbow Mountain with its multi-coloured sides. In the background lie the vast Kaingaroa Plains.

The Rotorua-Taupo thermal region has its own strange beauty, though hot springs can be found elsewhere in New Zealand. You will find boiling and ice-cold streams flowing side by side; the weird colours of mud and clay and sulphur rock; or a mud pool quaking like porridge in a bush clearing. The steam that rises from thermal vents can often be seen from far off. It is as if the too-often-neglected earth had suddenly shown aggression towards man, the anger of the Earth Mother.

PLATE 15
Waiotapu thermal area, looking towards
the Kaingaroa Plains.

THESE Douglas fir trees, in Whakarewarewa State Forest, a little south of Lake Rotorua, are typical of the many miles of planted forests that grow on the once barren volcanic plateau. In a certain measure the New Zealand Government, through its Forest Service, has atoned for the reckless devastation of native bush by the first European settlers. The wood of exotic conifers requires treatment for preservation against decay and insects, but they are fast-growing and provide a valuable source of timber. Indeed the quick growth of various species of pine in the New Zealand climate has provided the country with a new industry. The forests are cut down and pulped to feed the world's insatiable demand for newsprint.

The curse of the new forests is fire, lighted by careless campers, or even by the sun itself, when it happens to concentrate its rays through a piece of broken glass. Firebreaks have been made at regular intervals, men keep guard on high, raised platforms, while planes and helicopters are used for observation. But in the dry summer month fires do break out and are hard to control.

PLATE 16
Douglas firs beside the road through the
Whakarewarewa State Forest.

THIS is the Pohutu Geyser at Whakarewarewa, one of the finest in the region. By the gate of the Maori village visitors are met by licensed women guides, members of a unique profession. Children dive for coins in the shallow waters of the Puarenga Stream. The whole village is built on a crust of ground above the thermal caverns, and the Maoris use the boiling pools for both cooking and washing. It is no unusual thing for a householder to wake and find that a new steam vent has opened in his yard.

A path, fenced by carved posts, leads up past the Maori graveyard to the entrance of the maze of geysers and mud pools and silica terraces, and at its further end stands a model pa which reproduces the ancient kind of fortified village.

At the other side of the town of Rotorua, there is another Maori village called Ohinemutu. The carved interior of the Anglican church there is famous for its *tukutuku* panelling and carved woodwork.

PLATE 17
Pohutu Geyser, Whakarewarewa thermal area, Rotorua.

THIS is one of the many meeting-houses constructed and used by the sub-tribes of the Arawa Maoris. The powerful Arawa tribe occupied the land between Maketu in the Bay of Plenty and the Rotorua Lakes. "Te Takinga" is built on the neck of land between Lake Rotorua and Lake Rotoiti, in the township of Mourea.

The house itself, though of modern construction, is complete in its traditional details. On the gable is a carved figure (*tekoteko*) of the principal tribal ancestor—in this case Takinga, a warrior chief descended from Pikiao who founded the Ngati-Pikiao sub-tribe of the Arawas.

During and after the Maori Wars a large number of the great meeting-houses were destroyed or fell into disrepair. The present generation, however, has been called "the generation of the meeting-house", because so many Maori communities have re-erected their meeting-houses, often with the help of Government subsidies.

Sir Peter Buck, the Maori anthropologist, has written that the *whare whakairo* formed the peak of Maori architectural development. Each detail of carving and decoration has its symbolic meaning, embodying the legends and history of the tribe, and of the Maori race itself. The meeting-house and its *marae*—the courtyard in front of its porch—was the focal point of Maori social life and government; and at the present day, under changed circumstances, this is still true for many communities.

The Maoris, who seemed at the turn of the century a dying race, have now a high birth-rate, and share the work, dress and language of their European fellow-countrymen, without losing their own distinctive culture. Legal equality, inter-marriage, and the same basic education have put Maori and European New Zealanders on a common footing, though the problems of racial separation and assimilation are real ones. The building of tribal meeting-houses is one powerful factor in the handing-on of Maori arts to new generations, and when a finished house is opened to the public, with ritual ceremony, a new nerve-centre of Maori life comes into existence.

PLATE 18
"Te Takinga" Maori meeting-house,
Mourea, Rotorua.

HOLIDAY homes and pleasure craft crowd the shore of Okawa Bay, on Lake Rotoiti. This lake is joined to Lake Rotorua on the west by the Ohau Channel, and drains to the Bay of Plenty by the Kaituna River. In 1823 the Nga-Puhi chief, Hongi Hika, brought his canoes overland to Lake Rotoiti and proceeded to the island of Mokoia in Lake Rotorua where he launched a devastating surprise attack on the Arawa tribe. Along Hongi's Track, where the straining warriors pulled the canoes through bush and fern, a smooth tar-sealed motor-way runs now, though the same tall trees that looked down on Hongi still overshadow the road.

In 1864 the eastern part of the lake was the scene of a battle between the Arawas, loyal to the Government, and a band of supporters of the Maori King from the East Coast. Four hundred Arawas swept across Rotoiti in a flotilla of war canoes to establish a base in the palisaded pa of Komuhumuhu. Today the blue waters are disturbed only by the chug of launches and the creak of rowlocks.

PLATE 19
Okawa Bay, Lake Rotoiti, on the Rotorua-Tauranga highway.

ON the magnificent curve of Ohope Beach, four miles from Whakatane, sea foods are plentiful. It is a holiday resort backed by rich farmlands. Of such a place Keith Sinclair has written in his poem, "Ihumatao" . . .

Look from the meadows and the purple willows,
Where the beach fends off the wild-tongued
Sea from our metropolis, the grey host
Of the waves from our bright, crumbling enclosure . . .

This coast was named the Bay of Plenty by Cook, because his hungry ship cast anchor here and sailed away well provisioned by the friendly Maoris. Whakatane itself is almost a land-locked port. Maize is grown in the district and there are paper and board mills. Here in the shadow of Pohaturoa Rock, where the *Mataatua* canoe made landfall from Hawaiki, the chiefs of the Bay of Plenty signed the Treaty of Waitangi, handing over their sovereignty to Queen Victoria in exchange for Government protection.

SEA breakers with the shape of a bird's wing foam in on Makarori Beach north of Gisborne. The view looks from north to south. Makarori is typical of the many wild beaches of the East Coast, where the waves of the Pacific carve strange shapes in the rock, and the giant roots of the pohutukawa trees go down to the water's edge; and where the high peak of Hikurangi is lit by the rising sun, while land and ocean still wait restlessly in shadow for the dawn to come.

You can travel this coast for half a day and meet only a boy on a horse and a few stray cattle. But when the pohutukawa blossoms flare out like gunfire, it is the sign for city dwellers to pour this way in cars, with food and stoves and sun-tan lotion, to pitch their tents and park their caravans on the shore below the Maori farms.

PLATE 21
East Coast seascape; Makarori Beach from the road north of Gisborne.

THE imported poplar and the indigenous cabbage-tree frame this view of the bed of the Tukituki River, at Craggy Range, near Havelock North. Craggy Range itself is twelve miles by road from Hastings, the centre of a district engaged in farming, fruit-growing and nursery gardening.

There are few large buildings in the two major towns of the Hawke's Bay province, Hastings and Napier, since many buildings were razed by earth tremors in Napier and by fire in Hastings, in the disastrous earthquake of 1931. There is a bird sanctuary at Lake Tutira, twenty miles north of Napier, where a sheep-station owner, Guthrie-Smith, wrote his classic work on local flora and fauna. Bishop Bennett, a Maori and the first Anglican Bishop of Aotearoa, though a member of the Arawa tribe of Rotorua, made his home in Hawke's Bay.

PLATE 22
The Tukituki River and Craggy Range near Havelock North, Hawke's Bay.

H ERE Romney sheep are being mustered on the shores of Lake Runanga, near Fernhill, six miles north of Hastings. The familiar sight of man and horse and dog can be seen on every sheep-farm in New Zealand during mustering. His dogs are like a shepherd's extra limbs. Directed only by the sound of a distant whistle or shouted instructions that bear no resemblance to the English language, they will climb high spurs or scout long paddocks, bringing in recalcitrant sheep on their own.

The cross of Romney rams with Southdown ewes produces fat, strong lambs for the freezing works. There is no fixed price for wool and mutton, as there is for dairy produce; but since last century the economy of New Zealand has depended heavily on the export of refrigerated meat. In Hawke's Bay, as in parts of the South Island, the big sheep-station owners became perhaps New Zealand's only aristocracy, influential in provincial and national politics. Today the farms are smaller, but the sheep-farmer, unlike his "cow-cockie" neighbour, still has a life that allows some room for leisure, in spaces of the annual cycle of lambing, docking, drenching, shearing and dipping.

PLATE 23
Mustering along the Lake Runanga shores between Napier and Hastings.

THIS is the Paekakariki Beach, north of Wellington, showing the highway, and the settlements along the coast, where many workers in Wellington live, going daily to and from the Capital City by rail. Many also visit the beach in weekends or on holidays, for swimming, boating and fishing. The name Paekakariki means "the perching-place of the green parakeet".

The high offshore island of Kapiti is now a sanctuary for native birds. The warrior Te Rauparaha with his Ngati-Toa people, who migrated from Kawhia early in the last century, captured Kapiti about 1820. The islands and the rocks off its sheltered southern shore were bases for whalers also in those days. A Wellington poet, Alistair Campbell, in his poem, "Looking at Kapiti", has indicated the impression one gains of the island on a stormy night . . .

> Sleep, Leviathan, shouldering the Asian
> Night sombre with fear, kindled by one star
> Smouldering through fog, while the goaded ocean
> Recalls the fury of Te Rauparaha.
>
> Massive, remote, familiar, hung with spray,
> You seem to guard our coast, sanctuary
> To our lost faith . . .

By sunlight, on a clear day, it is a bold landmark only, sharpening to a silhouette as the sun sets in the sea beyond.

PLATE 24
Looking north from Paekakariki Hill along the coastline to South Manawatu.

THIS view shows Wellington City, the capital of New Zealand, though Auckland has always been ready to contend her title. Looking down from the Tinakori Hills, you can see in receding order the old wooden Government Buildings, modern blocks of offices, the railway station, the wharves, part of the harbour large enough to shelter a navy or two, houses on the steep hill-face above Oriental Bay, and a glimpse of the heads and the outer sea.

Wellington, founded in 1840, is becoming increasingly a city of suburbs. Beyond this picture, to the left, lies the Hutt Valley, where expanding industries have led to the growth of new housing areas. Perhaps Louis Johnson has caught the spirit of the suburbs best in his "Song in the Hutt Valley" . . .

Cirrus, stratus, cumulus,
Gentle or giant winds
Invoke the trees and cabbages;
The rising jet-trail finds
Space out of sight and valleys
Where the muddy rivers run
Past houses, groves and alleys
In the residential sun.
The placid eaves of evening
Purpled by homing sun
Take small account of reckoning
Broadcast by weatherman.
Houses still grow, the children
Like cabbages are seen;
Grandfather's thoughts are hidden
Upon the bowling green . . . .

PLATE 25
Wellington City and Harbour from
Tinakori Hill looking east.

THIS quiet sheep pasture at Clareville, north of Carterton, in the Wairarapa, could almost be an English country scene; though the corrugated iron roofs of the farmhouse and sheds are distinctively New Zealand. Carterton is a farming township with dairy factories, and small local industries. Less than twenty miles away stands Mount Holdsworth, a peak of the Tararua Range, of which C. K. Stead writes in his poem, "Night Watch in the Tararuas"...

Moon bathes the land ... throws shadows down
From thorn and manuka over the stunted ground ...
Rabbits thump their warnings through earth hard
As the carved gleam of Holdsworth against the sky,
Whose upright, white-capped miles catch the moon's eye ...

To reach the Wairarapa the road zig-zags up and down the steep flanks of the Rimutaka Range and crosses its windy crest. From the north it runs along the deep scoured gorges of the Manawatu and Makakaki Rivers.

PLATE 26
Wairarapa pastureland at Clareville, between
Masterton and Carterton.

OUR North Island sequence ends with a sunset over lagoon waters near Napier. These recurring colours of sky and water, seen by Cook and Tasman, by European settlers and a million Polynesian tribesmen before them, are unrelated to human endeavour. They have flamed impartially over births and battles and funerals; over the mission churches and the grog-shops of the whalers; over football crowds and farmers working late with tractor and plough, and civil servants hurrying to their trains.

They stand perhaps for what can only be known through silence and patience—a lucidity which man stands outside, an order greater than the human one. In a sense our sequence is made to direct your attention to this world in which we live but to which we so rarely belong.

PLATE 27
Sunset near Napier, Hawke's Bay.

FOR those who cross Cook Strait by the interisland ferry steamer, the Lyttelton Heads are one of the northern gates to the South Island . . . .

From open water moves the slug-like ferry
Towards the land's rough gates . . . .
Now inch by inch the angry ledges fall
Astern; brown floating weeds
Ride the bow wave. The harbour grows
    around us
With pinetree island, road and bungalow . . . .
The ship swings to the wharf
Toy-like with standing cars and cranes like
    giant moas . . . .
Steady the wind pours from its valley funnel
Above the town, cool terminus
Of many roads . . . .

This view of Lyttelton Harbour shows the heads clearly, and the open sea beyond, with the settlement at Governors Bay visible in the left foreground. The harbour cuts deep into the land, for the sea has breached the wall of the huge volcanic cone, once an island, that is Banks Peninsula. The immigrant ships with the early Canterbury settlers arrived here in 1850. Road and railway tunnels pierce the Port Hills at their narrowest part, leading through to the city of Christchurch and the Canterbury Plains.

PLATE 28
Lyttelton Harbour looking towards the heads.

THE River Avon winds through the city of Christchurch, its surface broken by trailing willow branches and diving ducks. Christchurch carries still, more perhaps than any other New Zealand town, the mark of English settlement. Eastward lie the marine suburbs of New Brighton and Sumner; westward and southward the flat farm country of the Canterbury Plains, sloping up to the foothills of the Southern Alps. This is the country of Samuel Butler's *Erewhon*, tussock land, where the big sheep-runs were established soon after European settlement.

In Cathedral Square, at the heart of Christchurch, stands the statue of John Robert Godley, founder of the province. Denis Glover, a South Island poet, has written aptly of the pioneers . . .

But if I sing of anything
I much prefer to sing of where
The tram-cars clang across the square,
Or where above the little bay
John Robert Godley passed his day,
Or where the brooding hills reveal
The sunset as a living weal.

I think, too, of the bridle-track
Where first they saw the plains curve back
To Alps, of how that little band
Of pilgrims viewed their Promised Land . . .

Practical men, yet troubled by dreams and ideals; Spartans and pilgrims who longed to graft a new shoot on the English tree. Perhaps they did not achieve their vision. But the vividly carved and painted interior of the Canterbury Provincial Building bears witness to them, and the many streets in Christchurch named after Church of England bishoprics.

PLATE 29
Christchurch. The Avon River winds
through the city and its parks.

THIS view from Fisherman's Wharf, shows the town of Kaikoura on the coastal route between Christchurch and Blenheim. Across the bay are the Seaward Kaikoura Mountains fresh with winter's early snows. The name Kaikoura has been abbreviated from "Te Ahi-kaikoura-a-Tama-ki-te-Rangi" which means "The fire in which Tama-ki-te-Rangi cooked crayfish". The cane crayfish pot in the foreground shows that this favourite food of the Maori is still available hereabouts in ample quantities.

The Kaikouras were sighted by Captain Cook, and named by him "The Lookers-On Mountains". Passing them by plane, or daylight ferry, you cannot fail to be impressed by their jagged, invulnerable heights. European settlement began with shore whaling in the early part of the last century. When excavations were made for the first house in the settlement, a moa's egg was discovered, the first intact egg to be found in New Zealand. It was sold later in England for a hundred guineas.

PLATE 30
The coastal township of Kaikoura on the
Christchurch-Blenheim road.

QUEEN Charlotte Sound, here seen from Queen Charlotte Drive, Marlborough, is the easternmost of the drowned valleys that comprise the Marlborough Sounds. Captain Cook, who named the sound, visited it three times to refit and repair his ship and refresh his crew.

Picton, which lies at the southern extremity of this sound, is the main export outlet for the Marlborough Province. From here a regular steamer service operates to and from Wellington, carrying in summer full cargoes of holiday-makers bound for the bush-clad bays, the blue water and the peace of "The Sounds"; or heading back home with memories of lazy days and energetic fishing trips.

Though the sound is here shown in a peaceful mood, winds can swoop down from the hills with little warning and raise storms dangerous to small boats. At such times the wise launch captain runs for shelter.

PLATE 31
In Queen Charlotte Sound.

HERE the morning frost still clings to the roadside grasses in the Kaituna Valley, on the main highway between Blenheim and Nelson. This is sheep country, north of the Wairau River. Of such places Denis Glover has written . . .

We, in the angle of a clock's hands,
Envy your country lives.

Therefore, beyond the city, we are glad to find
Your country, where the flat roads run
Like helter-skelter hares across the land,
With its frontier the capricious ford
And your fields that lie towards one another,
Mountains being near . . .

Fronting your formidable hills, hedges are toys
And toy-like those scattered buildings;
Nevertheless home to you,
And your wide gates stand open.

RIWAKA is in Nelson Province, and lies near the coast of Tasman Bay, on the fertile flats of the Riwaka Valley. Nearby is the larger township of Motueka and the two places are so fortunate in climate and soil that they provide all of the hops and tobacco grown in New Zealand, as well as vegetable and fruit crops. In the harvest season fields swarm with baked-brown migrant workers, and picking machines seem to float over the tall, green tobacco plants like Indian howdahs—without supporting elephants.

To the south east is the provincial centre, Nelson, a city favoured by sunshine and the prosperity of the surrounding countryside. North of Riwaka the Takaka Hill rises as an abrupt barrier, and its popular name of "The Marble Mountain" reminds us that the stone used for the Parliament Buildings in Wellington came from here.

The agricultural calm of the Motueka, Riwaka and Takaka valleys has its contrast in Abel Tasman National Park, which runs north from Kaiteriteri Beach to the Abel Tasman memorial plinth near Tarakohe. This stretch of tumbled hills and forested coastline, as beautiful as any in New Zealand, is well-known to Nelson folk but has yet to be "discovered" by most New Zealanders.

But its first discovery by Europeans was notable indeed. Abel Tasman hove to off Tarakohe in 1642, lost three of his men in a brush with the Maoris, and sailed away, never to set foot in the new land he had found. In 1827 the next explorer in these parts, the famous French navigator Dumont D'Urville, took shelter in Astrolabe Roadstead, a few miles north of Kaiteriteri.

PLATE 33
Riwaka Valley in the Nelson Province, looking towards Motueka.

A trace of early morning fog rests on the deep-flowing Buller River, close to Inangahua, on the highway between Nelson and Westport. The Buller River is one of New Zealand's largest, rising on the St. Arnaud and Spenser Mountains, and flowing westward to enter the Tasman Sea at Westport . . . .

Winds from the stormy Tasman
Bring rain; the lush, green bush
Receives their tribute in a net of leaves . . .

The Buller Gorge is in the Nelson Province, but further south lies Westland. The province of Westland, producing gold and coal and timber, as well as farm produce, has a very distinct character. The rainfall on the West Coast is heavy, because the Southern Alps, east of the narrow coastal area, catch the moisture-laden clouds brought by sea winds; and there is a lush growth of native bush, with streams and rivers that swell suddenly. The people of the West Coast are, in popular opinion, rugged and open-hearted, with a strong tendency to local autonomy.

PLATE 34
The Buller River near Inangahua, on the Nelson-Westport highway.

HERE we look south across Woodpecker Bay, on the Tasman coast between Westport, on the Buller River, and Greymouth, on the Grey. The road that links these West Coast towns follows some forty miles of rugged coastline.

Woodpecker Bay is of no commercial consequence today but a hundred years ago it served as one of the many makeshift ports that brought miners and supplies to the gold diggings of the Coast. Nearby Tiromoana, then known as Brighton, was the scene of a goldrush, and to the north were the boom towns of Charleston and Addisons.

Just to the south is Punakaiki, where occurs one of the most remarkable natural features of the West Coast: a limestone headland, its neck covered with bush and nikau palms, its rocks weathered in many places by the turbulent Tasman Sea to resemble piled-up heaps of pancakes, with caves, chasms and blowholes. The display of geyser-like jets is accompanied by a thundering noise in the caves, and in heavy weather the sight is worth coming many miles to see.

PLATE 35
Woodpecker Bay on the West Coast road between
Westport and Greymouth.

THE Franz Josef Glacier, twin glory and pride—with its neighbouring Fox Glacier—of South Westland, is here seen flanked by forest growth and reflected in Peter's Pool. This great river of ice is born in the snowfields of the Southern Alps, and descends about eight thousand feet in its eight-mile course, until it unfreezes at around seven hundred feet to form the Waiho River, which hustles over the narrow coastal plain and into the Tasman Sea.

In winter the ponderous movement is slowed but in the summer thaw the glacier looses its icy grip on the rock and moves in imperceptible majesty, groaning, rumbling and squealing as the vast mass yields to millions of tons of pressure above.

The glacier was named by its discoverer, the geologist von Haast, in honour of the then Emperor of Austria-Hungary. Peter's Pool was named for Peter Graham, one of two mountaineering brothers who pioneered routes and guided climbers up the peaks and across the passes of the Mt. Cook region.

PLATE 36
The terminal face of Franz Josef Glacier,
reflected in Peter's Pool.

THESE delicate beeches near Springs Junction, on the Lewis Pass highway between Reefton and Christchurch, are typical of the forest through which many South Island roads travel. Of trees such as these a New Zealand poet has written . . .

> Some few yards from the hut the standing beeches
> Let fall their dead limbs, overgrown
> With feathered moss and filigree of bracken.
> The rotted wood splits clean and hard
> Close-grained to the driven axe, with sound of water
> Sibilant falling and high nested birds.
>
> In winter blind with snow; but in full summer
> The forest blanket sheds its cloudy pollen
> And cloaks a range in undevouring fire . . .

The Lewis Pass route is an ancient one. East coast Maoris travelled this way across the Main Divide to obtain supplies of West Coast greenstone (jade) for their ornaments, tools and weapons, and to trade with North Island tribes.

There is another view of this region on the back of the jacket of this book.

PLATE 37
Beech forest on the Lewis Pass Road
near Springs Junction.

THE Rakaia River flows from the Main Divide to an outlet south of Banks Peninsula. This view shows an interesting terrace formation in the riverbed, near the Rakaia Gorge bridge, and indicates clearly the ancient river levels. The foothills of the Mount Hutt Range can be seen in the background. When the snows melt in the spring, the Rakaia, like other rivers fed from the Southern Alps, floods freely. Many of the first European settlers and gold prospectors, unused to the New Zealand rivers, lost their lives by drowning . . .

I camped on a shingle flat
Beside the loud Rakaia,
And drove my tent pegs in
And built a fire of dry manuka.

I'd bread in the saddlebags
And tea in the black billy
And enough tobacco to last me
All the way to Gabriel's Gully.

I stretched out like a log
Dreaming of girls and cider
And Death came like a riding man
With proud hooves of mountain water . . .

These foothills of the Southern Alps, tussock country, provide good grazing for sheep.

PLATE 38
The Rakaia River and the foothills of
Mount Hutt Range, Canterbury.

HERE not far from Burkes Pass, we see the darkness of a storm approaching over the tussock lands of the Mackenzie Country, in inland Canterbury. The Mackenzie Country takes its name from a Scottish Highland shepherd who discovered the pass in 1850 and promptly used it to spirit away flocks of sheep stolen from the landowners.

Ursula Bethell, in her poem *By Burke's Pass*, has left us a vigorous description of the place . . .

Nature, earth's angel, man's antagonist,
    The stern antagonist from whom he wrests his bread,
Long heretofore with vast magnificence
    Did carve this scene, prepare the arena, spread
Bronze tussocked terraces before precipitous
    Great purple alps, loose glacier-shed
Fierce-laughing streams in circuitous riverbed.

To her, as to me, the country seemed hostile as well as magnificent. But to the shepherd, McKenzie, already accustomed to the bare rocks of the Highlands, it may have seemed a friendly shelter, and its loneliness preferable to the company of those who eventually gaoled him.

PLATE 39
The Mackenzie Country; sheep grazing
lands in inland Canterbury.

SILVER birches show their bright autumn foliage in this view of Mt. Cook, New Zealand's highest mountain, seen from The Hermitage resort hotel. The Maori name for the peak was Aorangi, "cloud in the sky."

The mountain was first climbed on Christmas Day, 1894 by three young and inexperienced Canterbury men, who were determined that New Zealanders should reach the summit before an English mountaineer, who had come to New Zealand for the purpose, could claim it.

Mt. Cook rises 12,349 feet at the head of the Hooker Valley and dominates the Hermitage scene. Almost a thousand feet higher than Tasman, its highest neighbour, it stands among twenty of New Zealand's highest mountains, all of them over 10,000 feet.

The Hermitage and its attendant buildings form a little settlement in the heart of a magnificent alpine region. In summer mountaineers come to risk their lives in difficult ascents and ski-planes land skiers in the high snow-fields. Less venturesome folk have lower peaks and glaciers to explore, and tourists can walk through alpine valleys to lakes and lookout points, or obtain a bird's-eye view of the whole region in an hour's flight to the high summits, across the Main Divide, and back again.

PLATE 40
Mount Cook (12,349 ft.). A view taken from The Hermitage.

TYPICAL of the mountain lakes of the South Island is Ohau, close to the sky, ruffled by the wind that blows down from the tussock ranges. This view looks into the Dobson Valley at the head of the lake, with Glen Mary peak on the left, and the Ben Ohau Range, glittering with the first snows, on the right.

Ohau stands higher than her sister lakes, Pukaki and Tekapo, within the grip of the Southern Alps. Her waters are crystal-clear, home of the silver-bellied eels. On her shores grow manuka and matagouri, the grey thorn-bush; and a number of mountain streams flow down through pool and cataract into her shingle basin. Here you can camp among the flowering manukas, lay lines for the eels (which taste better than trout if they are first boiled, to remove the fat, and then fried) or perhaps shoot a hare and cook it Maori-style in a pit with hot stones on the lake shore.

PLATE 41
Lake Ohau and the Dobson Valley looking towards
Glen Mary and the Ben Ohau Range.

AT the Lindis Pass the main inland highway running along the foothills of the Southern Alps reaches a height of 3,185 feet above sea level. This view looks westwards over the endless tussock-lands.

The bareness and wide spaces of Central Otago, the clear light and treeless hillsides, give the traveller the impression that he is entering some kingdom of the elements quite uninhabited by men. As one New Zealand poet has written . . .

Alone we are born
And die alone,
Yet see the red-gold cirrus
Over snow mountain shine.

Upon the upland road
Ride easy, stranger.
Surrender to the sky
Your heart of anger.

PLATE 42
In the Lindis Pass which links Canterbury and Otago.
View looking westwards.

HERE the view is south, looking over the swift waters of the Clutha River, from the main inland highway between Tarras and Cromwell. The three main source lakes of this river are Hawea, Wanaka and Wakatipu, and for its length it has as large a flow of water as any river in the world. One of the great water-dragons of the South Island, it rises periodically and floods the farms that lie alongside its banks in the coastal area. Its grimmer aspect has been celebrated in New Zealand verse . . .

Iron cages cross on a rope
The wide river whose musical coils,
Older than Charybdis, wrap
Boulders, bodies, and blue eels.

The iron cages are the chairs slung on a wire cable, relics of goldrush days, which are still used here and there to cross the gorges of the Clutha where there is no bridge. It is a remarkable spectacle to see at Cromwell the blue water of the Clutha and the water of the Kawarau join and mingle. Twenty miles downstream is the major junction, where the Clutha absorbs the Manuherikia at Alexandra, and twenty more miles along, at Roxburgh, the flow has been massively dammed for the generation of power.

PLATE 43
The Clutha River between Tarras and Cromwell, Central Otago.

L AKE Wakatipu, the longest of the Southern Lakes, is shaped somewhat like an elongated "S". Like the mountain lakes of Switzerland and Northern Italy, it is of glacial origin, and the terminal moraine of the ancient glacier formed the land where Kingston now stands. In this view one sees the jagged slopes of the Remarkables, which extend along the eastern shore of the lake, clothed with snow and sunlight and a few clouds.

Queenstown, on the shores of a bay on the eastern side, is the headquarters of those who come for sight-seeing. In the early days of settlement sailing craft were used on the lake; today there is an aged and elegant lake steamer, and motor launches. The bridge across the outlet where Lake Wakatipu flows into the Kawarau River runs across a set of locks built to lower the level of the river for the more efficient working of alluvial gold deposits. The dam failed to hold back the waters and not an ounce of gold was won by its use.

Ski-ing grounds have been developed at Coronet Peak, about twelve miles from the town by way of Skippers Road.

PLATE 44
Lake Wakatipu and the Remarkables
from near Queenstown.

THE Shotover River is seen here in a golden light that reminds us of the gold that was won from its shingle a hundred years ago. Queenstown was then the centre of a rush that brought thousands of men to the river gorges and the lonely creek beds. Thomas Arthur, who gave his name to Arthurs Point, the scene of this photograph, took two hundred ounces of gold from the river sands of the Shotover in eight days, and four thousand pounds worth in two months.

Denis Glover has written a sprightly "Holiday Piece" about this area . . .

> Now let my thoughts be like the Arrow
>     wherein was gold,
> And purposeful like the Kawarau
>     but not so cold.
>
> Let them sweep higher than the hawk
>     ill-omened,
> Higher than peaks perspective-piled beyond
>     Ben Lomond;
> Let them be like at evening an Otago sky
> Where detonated clouds in calm confusion lie.
>
> Let them be smooth and sweet as all those
>     morning lakes,
> Yet active and leaping, like fish the
>     fisherman takes;
> And strong as the dark deep-rooted hills,
>     strong
> As twilight hours over Lake Wakatipu are
>     long.

PLATE 45
The Shotover River on the
Queenstown-Arrowtown Road.

THE road from Queenstown to Skippers rises 3,000 feet and snakes around 480 bends, all in matter of fourteen miles, and the excursion is as noted for its spine-chilling bends and precipices as for the grandeur of its scenery. This photograph shows the narrow road, with Lighthouse Rock in the foreground.

Skippers once swarmed with diggers. In a matter of years every square yard of soil was washed or sifted, every pebble scrutinised, every cranny explored—but no one values its lonely valleys now. Only ruined buildings and rusted machinery remain to comfort the ghosts of eight thousand miners who fought for the yellow fruits of its otherwise barren hills. The last of the miners died only a few years ago, a victim of the snow and the freezing cold that claimed so many of his fellows in the 1860s.

PLATE 46
Skippers, looking along the valley;
Lighthouse Rock in foreground.

THE moment of success is captured, as a fisherman nets a trout in the Eglinton River, a hundred yards from the shore of Lake Te Anau.

The lake is the South Island's largest and a holiday resort in its own right, as well as a staging post on the route to Milford Sound. Launches explore its bush-clad waterways and visit its glow-worm caves. The Eglinton Valley narrows northwards between mountain ranges, and a few miles south is Manapouri, "the lake of a hundred islands". From the head of the lake the Milford Track provides an easy three- or four-day walk to Milford Sound.

Across Te Anau is Fiordland, where no men live (except at Milford Sound) and where only hunters and trampers venture. But the Murchison Mountains, in the background, are home to an important community, the sole remaining colony of the flightless notornis, which was discovered in 1948 and has been carefully protected since.

The Murchisons separate the glacial valleys of the lake's South and Middle Fiords. To the west, fiords of similar origin, but which are called sounds, bring the sea into the heart of the mountains so that, as the amphibian flies, there is a mere ten miles between fresh water and salt. But any-one who knows the Fiordland terrain and weather, and its annual rainfall of 250 or more inches, will laugh at the phrase "a *mere* ten miles".

PLATE 47
The Eglinton River near the shore
of Lake Te Anau.

THE precipices of Mount Talbot tower above the head-
waters of the Hollyford River, near the Homer Saddle.
In his remarkable elegy for a friend killed in the Southern Alps, Alistair Campbell has described the Hollyford
Valley in winter . . .

Storm. Storm in the trees,
Everywhere the hidden sound
Of water, like hives of bees
Up-tilted, deep underground.

The shattered cliff's sheer
Face spurts myriads
Of waterfalls, like tears
From some deep-bowed head

Whose colossal grief is stone,
Great trees rooted fast
In ice, nightlong moan
Down the gleaming pass . . . .

The Homer Saddle has been part of the route to Milford
Sound for over fifty years. Mountaineers who tramped up
the Eglinton and Hollyford Valleys would ascend the saddle,
work their way around the Grave-Talbot Pass, and descend
to Milford by a circuitous route.

A 63-chain tunnel under the saddle was begun in 1935 and
opened to traffic in 1954, thus completing the road link that
commenced as a Depression project at Te Anau in 1929.
Except in the savage months of winter, when the avalanche
risk is high, the road remains open and its 74 miles constitute
probably the finest scenic highway in New Zealand.

PLATE 48
Mount Talbot in the Upper Hollyford Valley
on the road to Milford Sound.

F AMOUS Mitre Peak rises more than five thousand feet directly from the waters of Milford Sound, and the flank of the mountain occupies almost all of the fiord's southern wall. As New Zealand's most distinctive and publicised landmark it never fails to impress, or to dominate the scene. There is power in its upthrusting ridge, grace in the final sweep to the summit, loneliness in its noble crown, and a variety of moods that follow changes in the weather and in the day or night sky.

The little promontory in the foreground is Cemetery Point, the delta of the Bowen Falls, which thunder 530 feet down a rock face from the valley of an ancient glacier. All this is "glacier country". The near-vertical, scarred mountainsides and the narrow valleys that twist to the sea are plain evidence of an era when ice was the master of granite.

Fragile toetoe grows among the foreshore boulders and the forest behind is predominantly beech. The word "fiord" means a threshold in Norwegian, and Milford is a true threshold to the northern fastnesses of Fiordland. Maoris knew its loneliness, for they came here for tangiwai, the "tear-drop" greenstone. Europeans first visited in 1823, and in 1877 Donald Sutherland, "the hermit of Milford Sound", arrived and stayed on until he died, 42 years later. His accommodation house has been replaced by a fine government hotel.

PLATE 49
Mitre Peak, Milford Sound.

IN 1844 the Chief Surveyor of the New Zealand Company reported on Southland and described it as "a mere bog and unfit for habitation". He was proved wrong. In 1861 Southland became a separate province; but after financial difficulties rising from a disastrous flood and an attempt to construct railways with wooden rails, the young province was re-united with Otago. Southland is chiefly a centre of extensive primary industries—agriculture, pasture and timber, served by the city of Invercargill, which has an air of confident prosperity and by the expanding port of Bluff, where there are commercial sea fisheries and oyster-canneries.

Here is a view of sheep-raising country between Lumsden and Dipton. In the distance stand the Hokonui Hills, where, according to popular report, illicit whisky stills have operated and may still operate. Lumsden, approximately forty miles from Invercargill, is close to the Oreti River, a singularly lovely stream which rises in the mountains west of Lake Wakatipu and flows south to enter Foveaux Strait.

PLATE 50
Southland pasturelands between Lumsden and Dipton, en route to Invercargill.

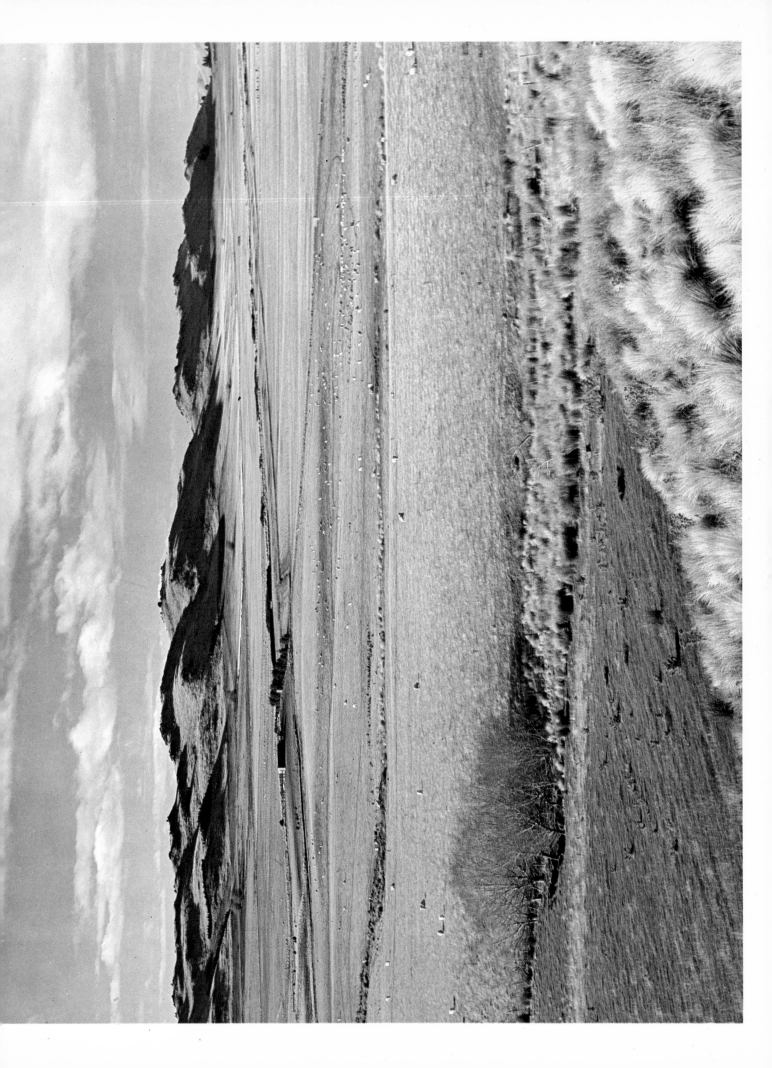

THIS view shows part of Dunedin city and harbour, from near the observatory. The Otago Province was founded by immigrants from Scotland in 1848. In the city many traces of Scotland still remain—in the names of streets, the University with its heavy grey clock-tower, the Leith Stream that flows over cylindrical weirs, and the statue of Robert Burns sitting thoughtfully in the Octagon, with his back to the Cathedral and his face to the Oban Hotel.

> Under Flagstaff's boulders
> Beds the town; and the houses
> Complacent over one another's shoulders
> Look on a harbour pleasant as a pond
> —With gate-crashing rollers just beyond
> Where remotely the sugared island still
> Winters in the Pacific's hug and maul.
>
> Over the harbour waters
> A slow-gonged clock
> Floats the hours and the quarters.
>
> From the quarry, all day without shock
> Comes the hill-deadened, water-damped
> Sounds of explosions; and haunting
> The frost-quiet of midnight
> The redundant the echoing
> Bull-breath of shunting . . .
>
> A long sunset spills
> On those returning
> And the manuka hills
> Know the slow smoke of burning.

More clearly than any visual artist Denis Glover has caught the life-rhythm of Dunedin in these lines.

PLATE 51
Dunedin City and harbour from the vicinity
of the observatory.

THIS last view shows Karitane Beach and headland, on the eastern coastal route between Dunedin and Oamaru.

The waves move in from the cold Pacific; the trees go down to the water's edge. Karitane is now a farming community and a holiday resort but it has been a place of consequence in Maori history and the scene of early European labours in Otago. A fortified Maori village on the little peninsula successfully withstood a siege of many months; whalers, the first Pakehas to settle, established shore stations in these bays and they were followed by a mission settlement.

Our photographic sequence now comes to an end. It began at Cape Reinga, the ancestral departing-place for the spirits of the Maori dead, traversed the North and South Islands of New Zealand, and closes at Karitane, where Maori and Pakeha have lived for many years at peace together. We hope we have revealed to you in some measure the contours of these islands, the human City and the natural Wilderness.

PLATE 52
Karitane Beach and headland on the
Dunedin-Oamaru route.

# ACKNOWLEDGMENTS

Quotations in this book from the works of New Zealand poets are gratefully acknowledged to:

CAXTON PRESS. "By Burke's Pass" by Ursula Bethell from *Collected Poems;* "Dunedin Revisited" from Sings Harry and other Poems, "Holiday Piece", "Letter to Country Friends" and "Home Thoughts" from *The Wind and the Sand* all by Denis Glover; "Sharemilkers" by Barry Mitcalfe and "Night Watch in the Tararuas" by C.K. Stead, both from *Landfall;* and "Ihumatao" by Keith Sinclair from *Strangers and Beasts.*

PEGASUS PRESS. "Looking at Kapiti" from *New Zealand Poetry Year Book* and "Hollyford Valley" from *Mine Eyes Dazzle,* both by Alistair Campbell; and "Song in the Hutt Valley" by Louis Johnson from *New Zealand Poetry Year Book.*

NEW ZEALAND UNIVERSITY PRESS. "Dominion" by A.R.D. Fairburn from *Three Poems.*

OTHER QUOTATIONS are from issues of *New Zealand Poetry Year Book* published by A.H. & A.W. Reed and from the published and previously unpublished work of James K. Baxter. Some of his verses were written for *New Zealand In Colour.*

## NEW ZEALAND IN COLOUR—VOLUME TWO

A second extensive tour of New Zealand was undertaken by Kenneth and Jean Bigwood to obtain colour photographs for their second book. Although identical in format with *Volume One,* its coverage is essentially different, a contrast and complement to the first collection. The text has been written by author mountaineer John Pascoe.